Who Is Responsible For Sickness?

by Elbert Willis

Contents

This is one of the questions that you will have to settle. God told me there was going to be a doctor crisis. And there is today. Maybe you have read in the papers about doctors who, because of the problems with insurance, are backing up. Also many of the doctors are overloaded with so much work they cannot get to all their patients. They are trying right now to train some of the nurses and other people to take care of some of what they consider smaller things. But I want to say this to you as a word from the Lord that you haven't seen anything yet like you are going to see. I want to recommend to you that you learn how to believe God for your healing. Because there will come a time when there will be so much sickness in this country, that the doctors will be over-worked and many of you, because you are Christians, will be at the end of the line. The devil will see to that.

There are men and women dying in the hospital waiting rooms today. They are in the emergency room sometimes hours before they can get emergency treatment. There is a doctor crisis and it's going to get worse. This should not make you afraid, but it should make you realize that Jesus Christ wants you to accept Him as your healer.

Most of you have accepted Jesus as your Saviour. You've accepted Him as your Baptizer, as your Deliverer. I'm going to believe that you are going to come to the place, if you haven't already, *where you will accept Jesus as your Physician.*

I want to recommend my doctor to you. He's never out on call. He never has to go back for any refresher courses. He knows the cure for every disease. There is no new disease that comes up that He has to research to find out what to do with it. His name is Jesus Christ the Son of God.

Every one has a choice. You can go by medical healing or you can go by divine healing. I want you to realize that medical healing and divine healing are not the same. You have a choice. You can receive a healing through medicine or drugs, or you can learn how to get your healing from Jesus Christ the Son of God.

You can be saved and you can use a doctor all of your life and I'll see you in heaven. It will not keep you out of heaven. It will just keep you from getting some extra miracles down here. But I want to help you settle some questions in your heart about divine healing.

JOHN 10:10 says "THE THIEF COMETH NOT, BUT FOR TO STEAL, AND TO KILL, AND TO DESTROY: I AM COME THAT THEY MIGHT HAVE LIFE, AND HAVE IT MORE ABUNDANTLY." Jesus has not come to steal, kill and destroy. Any time you are sick you are being stolen from. You can't work on the job like you ought to when you are sick. You cheat your boss when you are sick. You may be out there punching the clock, but you are not as effective. When you moms are sick, you cheat your husband, you cheat your family, you cheat the kids. Oh, you can do the housework, but you're not as effective. You boys and girls cheat in school when you're sick. You can't do the studying, you can't do the work.

Whenever disease is attacking your body and the enemy has you sick then you cannot function effectively. So, therefore, he's stealing from you. He's killing you. You have to exert extra energy and extra strength to be able to make it from one day to the next. But Jesus has come that you might have life and have it more abundantly. And that means health.

MATTHEW 6:10 says "THY KINGDOM COME, THY WILL BE DONE IN EARTH, AS IT IS IN HEAVEN." Is there going to be any sickness in heaven? Well, then, you don't have to have it down here. "Oh, but Brother Willis, I believe I do have to have it down here." Then you'll have it. Divine healing is only for believers, those who believe they can be healed.

Many Christians tell me, "Brother Willis, I don't believe that God can heal."

And I say, "Don't worry. He won't heal you."

They say, "Well, what can I do?"

And I say, "Go to the doctor."

I believe that He will heal me because He's healed me many times. *You can only receive from God what you can believe Him for.* The Bible is clear and plain in that it is His will to heal you. That's His will. *Now if your will is not in line with His will, don't blame Him and don't blame the Word of God.* It's time that God's people began to wake up and quit taking part of the Bible, and realize that when Jesus Christ died at Calvary He died that you might be set free *spiritually, physically, mentally* and *financially*.

If you'll look in a Greek dictionary or concordance, you will see that the word "*sozo*" means saved, healed, delivered. It means all of it. We have spiritualized it. But the word "*save*" in the Bible does not mean just spiritually. The definition of the word is *spiritually, physically, made whole, delivered.* I thank God that I believe this.

So He says "THY KINGDOM COME. THY WILL BE DONE IN EARTH AS IT IS IN HEAVEN." Everything you can have in heaven, you can have a taste of down here. You need to be taught how to believe God. HEBREWS 11:6 says "WITHOUT FAITH IT IS IMPOSSIBLE TO PLEASE GOD."

How can you please Him if you don't know how to get your healing? How can you please Him if you don't know how to get your needs met?

Who is responsible for sickness? I would not debate this with you for thirty seconds. You can take the scripture or you can leave it. It's time that God's people who fly under the banner of Jesus Christ the Son of God quit saying, "I know the Bible says it, but..."

God's Word is still true regardless of what you think about it. *I thank God that His Word is not based upon us believing it.* Because if His Word had been based upon us believing I never would have gotten the Holy Spirit. Because I didn't believe it. I thought tongues were just for those emotional people and

Pentecostals; maybe the people that were not too well educated. In fact I didn't even know if it was for them.

As for divine healing I was so smart I thought God had sent doctors here to heal. I'm going to show you scripture to disprove that.

Do you know why more people haven't believed in divine healing? *It has not been taught. We've been taught salvation, so we believed in salvation, but we have never been taught divine healing.*

It's God's will for you to be healthy and whole. You may not be able to walk into that health immediately. Or God may give you a miracle. But if He doesn't give you a miracle, then you will recover. He said believers shall lay hands on the sick and they shall recover. Recovery is a progressive thing.

I. DISEASE WAS NOT PART OF GOD'S ORIGINAL CREATION PLAN

GENESIS 1:31 says "GOD SAW EVERYTHING HE HAD MADE, BEHOLD IT WAS VERY GOOD." I've never been sick when it was good. How about you? I didn't know anything good about it. It hurt. It was miserable. Have you ever had your throat all stopped up and it was good? Your nose all runny and it was good? Your stomach cramping and it was good? There wasn't anything good about it.

GENESIS 3:1 says "THE SERPENT WAS MORE SUBTLE THAN ANY BEAST OF THE FIELD WHICH THE LORD HAD MADE." He was cunning. He was crafty. He was apt. He was very skilled. He was very clever. He hated God because he had lost his high position. He began to behold his beauty and admire himself and became lifted up in pride. God spotted the pride in him and kicked him out.

God made man and when God made man, Satan hated man because man was made in the image of God. Man was coming closer to God than Satan ever had been when he was one of the angels in the glories of heaven. So he hated man. He still hates man. He began to plot and plan how he was going to steal from man that which God had given him.

If you'll read the Bible you'll find there never was an indication that there was sickness in the Garden of Eden. They had immortal life. They were free from disease. So everything God created in the garden was good. No disease. No sickness. You'll find out the disease and sickness did not come until sin came. *Disease and sickness came with the sin of Adam and Eve and freedom from sickness came with the death and resurrection of Jesus Christ the Son of God.* He more than outdid what the devil did. So you and I through the death and resurrection of Jesus Christ and through the power of the Holy Spirit that's in us can walk free of sickness and disease.

It won't be easy. The devil will come against you. He'll fight you. But if you'll start working on this thing and learn it it will be beautiful. There hasn't been an aspirin in our home since 1971. We have five children. Oh, he's knocked on our door. But we don't take his packages any more.

I had a stomach problem for five years. I couldn't keep Coke and crackers down, but the power of God healed my stomach and I went home and had the wife cook me some cabbage and corn bread. The devil said, "If you eat that stuff, you'll die." I used to pass by it and smell it and my stomach would get upset. That day she cooked that cabbage and I cut a piece of that corn bread and laid it down on the plate and covered it with cabbage. I got some vinegar and I doused it down real good and sat there and ate it. And when I got through the devil said, "You'll die."

I said, "Devil, you're a liar. Jesus has healed me. I'm not going to put up with this any more. I'm not going to have it any more. The Bible says that He that is within me is greater than he that is in the world. Jesus bore my sicknesses." And I walked right on out of that thing and can eat anything. Nothing bothers me any more. And every time I eat, I remind the devil. I say, "Devil, look."

Disease was not of God's original plan. And He's no respecter of persons, dear Christian friend. You have the same rights and privileges that I have.

II. DISEASE CAME AS A RESULT OF MAN'S FALL

1. MAN'S AUTHORITY. It says in GENESIS 1:26-28 that man would "HAVE DOMINION OVER" everything. And God through the death of Jesus Christ is bringing his people back to this authority. The Bible said that Jesus Christ more than overcame what the devil had done.

GENESIS 1:26 says "AND GOD SAID LET US MAKE MAN IN OUR IMAGE." Do you think he made him sick? Do you think he made him with a fever, with the flu, with the mumps, with the chicken-pox, ulcers, or a bad heart? Do you think he made him that way? No. He didn't make any one sick. The devil perverted the whole deal.

This amazes me. People talk about Jesus being a God of love. Can you picture a God of love making a little baby come out of the womb all deformed? Do you know who's the author of that? The devil. And the quicker we realize it the quicker we can start stopping some of these things. If I had known then what I know now my son Lynn would have never been born malformed. A lot of you have physical problems and malfunctions in your body that you were born with. I want to tell you, the devil did it. Jesus Christ wants to make you whole.

He says in that 26th verse that man would have dominion over the fowls of the air, over every creeping thing. In the 28th verse it says he would have dominion over the fish of the sea and over every living thing that moved upon the earth. God gave man authority and power over everything.

PSALMS 8:6 says "THOU MADEST HIM TO HAVE DOMINION OVER THE WORKS OF THY HAND, THOU HAST PUT ALL THINGS UNDER HIS FEET." When God made man, He put man in charge. Man was God's prime specimen. But the devil has perverted things and he's taken God's people and torn them down. He's got them defeated and frustrated and fearful and sick. But there's a mighty move of the Holy Spirit across this land today and people's eyes are beginning to be opened and they are beginning to realize that Jesus has redeemed them from the curse of the law. They don't have to be sick any more. They can be free in the name of Jesus. They have found out that Jesus Christ bought it all back at Calvary. He didn't buy just part of it back. He bought it all back.

What was man's authority? He had dominion over everything. The work that Jesus Christ has done today gives you and I dominion over these things.

2. MAN'S ABILITY. GENESIS 2:19 says "AND OUT OF

THE GROUND THE LORD GOD FORMED EVERY BEAST OF THE FIELD, AND EVERY FOWL OF THE AIR: AND BROUGHT THEM UNTO ADAM TO SEE WHAT HE WOULD CALL THEM: AND WHATSOEVER ADAM CALLED EVERY LIVING CREATURE, THAT WAS THE NAME THEREOF."

The scripture says that Adam named every living thing. That old boy was pretty smart. God trusted him. He had confidence in him. Through the Holy Spirit today God is restoring man's ability to be in control over disease and sickness.

All of you that are saved have the ability of God. You have the ability of Christ living inside of you and can take back dominion of those things that the enemy has taken away from you.

God had confidence in his creation. He does today in his new creation. II CORINTHIANS 5:17 says we become new creatures in Christ. He has a lot of confidence in us. He says in LUKE 10:19 "I GIVE YOU POWER AND AUTHORITY OVER ALL THE POWER OF THE ENEMY AND NOTHING SHALL BY ANY MEANS HURT YOU." That's how much confidence He has in you and I. He sent His son Jesus to live and die, He was raised from the grave and ascended back to the heavens, and He sent the Holy Spirit to live in you and I and now He says "I GIVE YOU POWER."

Every one of you have power and authority over all the power of the enemy. Not just a few people, but every single one of you.

3. HOW DID SATAN GET HIS AUTHORITY & POWER? The Bible very plainly teaches us that God put Adam in charge of everything. He gave him dominion over everything. He

named all the animals. This took tremendous ability and a tremendous mind.

Scientists say that we have a large brain and only a small part of it is being used. I believe Adam used all of it. But the devil has perverted man and man is just using about 20% of it today. I believe in these last days God is going to activate our brains so we can learn the Word of God. Just think if all of us could remember the Bible from cover to cover, anything the devil said to us, we could just quote him scripture, from Genesis to Revelation. He says if you will delight yourself in the Lord, He will give you the desires of your heart. One of my desires is to know the Bible from cover to cover. How did Satan get the authority? It says in LUKE 4:6-7 "IT HATH BEEN DELIVERED UNTO ME." Adam had it. God gave it to Adam and now we find in Luke that Satan had it. *When was it transferred*? Why did they turn loose of such a possession? If you today had a mind like Adam had, walked with God in the garden, named all the fowls of the air and the beasts of the field, would you turn loose of such a possession as that? What did Satan bargain or tempt him with?

GENESIS 3:5 says that Satan came to Eve and said "YE SHALL BE AS GODS, KNOWING GOOD AND EVIL." That means the devil with his shrewdness and his craftiness had to offer them something that looked better. The devil said, "Now, listen Eve. You and Adam walk in the garden. You are in charge. You've named all the animals here. You're number one. You have perfect life. You have everything. But you know there's something you don't have. You are not like God. You don't know the difference in good and evil. If you eat of that tree right over there, then you'll be like a god."

In her mind she began to comprehend how it would be to be like God. And the next thing you know she quit eating of the tree of life and went over and ate of the tree of good and evil. She then gave some to Adam and he ate. *When they entered into the snare of the devil, they fell into his trap, they came under his dominion and authority. They lost the ability and the power that they had when they sold out to the devil.*

And we find in Luke that the devil tells Jesus "Look out there at all the world. It's mine." So, therefore, in the fall in the Garden, Adam and Eve transferred dominion over to the devil. That's bad isn't it? *But don't forget a man named Jesus came and bought it back.* But most Christians don't know that they've got it back. Most Christians are walking in darkness today and they still think the devil's in control. They don't know that the Bible tells us that the devil has been defeated.

Jesus came to destroy the works of the devil. I believe he succeeded. Most of God's people have been kept in ignorance as to what their inheritance is. They think the devil is still greater than them. But the Bible says in I JOHN 4:4 that He that is in you is greater than he that is in the world. That means the power that God has put inside of you is greater than the power of the devil and when you begin to know who you are and what you are then you are going to begin to walk in your inheritance.

If you don't know your inheritance you can't do any good. Do you know what it reminds me of? Here in South Louisiana for many years the people lived in poverty. Living in shacks and travelling up and down the bayous in small boats.

And all the time there were billions of dollars of black gold underneath them. But they didn't know it. *Today in America there are many Christians in many of our churches with the power of God inside of them, but they don't know what they have.* They are still living in physical, mental and financial poverty. They are saved and going to heaven, but they have not yet found out what their inheritance is.

4. THE OUTCOME. Satan deceived them. Eve fell for it and went and ate of the tree. She went back and talked to Adam, and he listened to her, and went and ate of the tree. Adam was not deceived, he just disobeyed God outright.

What was the outcome of it? GENESIS 3:19 says "TILL THOU RETURN UNTO THE GROUND FOR OUT OF IT WAST THOU TAKEN, FOR DUST THOU ART AND UNTO DUST THOU SHALL RETURN." As a result of sin, death came. There was no death prior to that time. *So death came with sin. There was no sickness in the Garden. So sickness came with sin.* And Jesus came that you and I might be redeemed. That we might be saved, spiritually, physically, mentally and financially.

Prior to that time Adam and Eve walked with God in the garden. God instructed them and he spoke to them. But when they disobeyed God, they sinned. They turned over their authority and their control to the devil. God no longer walked with them and spoke with them. They no longer had God to guide them. So, therefore, they had to make it on their own. So that's when logic and reason began to develop. Their body had to be fed and they had to get out and do it. Prior to that time God was taking care of them. But after God quit taking care of them, because of their disobedience, their reason and their five senses developed. Everything they received from that day forward had to be gotten on their own. Ever since then the devil has been telling man that he has to get it himself.

These are the ways that Satan could influence them. Through their eyes, their nose, their mouth and their ears and their feelings. So he began to influence and control them, but it got to where their body cried out for this, and their mind cried out for this and soon they couldn't hear from God because their senses, logical and reason and their bodies began to take control. And this is where most Christians are today. If their body hurts, they go by their body. The Bible says you're healed. But your body says you're sick. You have two truths. A spiritual truth that says you were healed at Calvary. A natural truth says that you are sick. What happens? You begin to compute with your logic and reason and you let your logic and reason override the Word of God. So, therefore, you say you're sick.

Ever since the fall, man's mind has begun to control. So what is in your computer is what the world has put in your computer. *The world* has told you as you start getting older you are going to start getting sicker. *The world* has told you that you have to get old and sick and die. The Bible says it's appointed unto man once to die. "But, Brother Willis, if I don't get sick and die, how am I going to die?" God can just reach down here and turn off the motor. He started the motor; he can turn it off. But if you let him, the devil will turn your motor off with some disease or some sickness. And God wants to turn your motor off with His hand. I've made up my mind that the devil's not going to turn my motor off. He didn't turn it on. God is the author of life.

You go around today to your churches and say, "I want to tell you, if you'll receive Jesus Christ as healer, you'll never have to use a doctor again."

They'll say "You're crazy. You're nuts. You're a fanatic. That's stupid. That's ignorant. Everybody knows that God put doctors here." But doctors are not for believers. Doctors are for the lost, to keep them alive until we can get the message to them and get them saved.

You go in hospitals today and the first thing they want to know is your denomination. Jesus is your Saviour, your Lord, and your Master, and you walk into the hospital, and the first thing they say is, "What denomination are you?" Boy, that's a testimony isn't it? "My God can do anything, *but* heal my arthritis. My God can do anything, *but* take care of my varicose veins. My God can do anything, *but* heal my kidneys. My God is so mighty and so powerful, He's going to raise me from the grave, *but* He can't heal my tonsils. My God, I want to tell you when the trumpet sounds I am going to come out of that grave. I'm going to that place in the sky where there will be no more sickness, no more worry, no more frustration. My God is all mighty. My God is all powerful, *but* he can't take care of a toothache."

III. A DIVIDED HOUSE CANNOT STAND

MARK 3:22-26 says, "AND THE SCRIBES WHICH CAME DOWN FROM JERUSALEM SAID, HE HATH BEELZEBUB, AND BY THE PRINCE OF THE DEVILS CASTETH HE OUT DEVILS. AND HE CALLED THEM UNTO HIM, AND SAID UNTO THEM, IN PARABLES, HOW CAN SATAN CAST OUT SATAN? AND IF A KINGDOM BE DIVIDED AGAINST ITSELF, THAT KINGDOM CANNOT STAND. AND IF SATAN RISE UP AGAINST HIMSELF, AND BE DIVIDED, HE CANNOT STAND BUT HATH AN END."

If the devil is divided against himself, then he can't stand. Well, the same principle is with Jesus. If Jesus makes you sick and then goes around healing you, He's fighting Himself all the time. Most of the religious world today believes that they are sick because it is God's will. I've had a lot of them tell me, "Brother Willis, it's just God's will for me to be in this wheel chair. I'm glorifying God in this wheel chair."

And I say, "You are? Why don't you ask God to put your son or daughter in there so both of you can glorify God?"

I've had people tell me, "Well, I just believe it's the Lord's will for me to have this cancer."

And I just say, "You believe it is? Are you going to glorify God with that cancer? Well, why don't you ask God to give one to your husband, then?"

And if you believe it's God's will for you to be sick, *why are you going to a doctor trying to get well*? You are going against God's will. If Jesus made you sick, you ought to ask Him to make you a little sicker. Really it's utterly ridiculous the way the religious world today thinks about healing. They believe God is the author of sickness and they are going around trying to get man to heal them of what God gave them.

Dear Christian friend, if you'll just start using your head and just think for a moment, you will see that the devil has had people blinded. When I first began a long time ago to look at this thing and wonder about it, I would go to the hospitals and pray for the people who were sick. I used to tell some of them, "We're going to pray and ask God to heal you."

And they'd say, "Well, Brother Willis, that's all right, but I don't know if it's God's will to heal me or not. Honey, hand me my pill."

And I used to think how can they not know if it's God's will to heal them and take medicine to heal them. *If you don't know if it's God's will to heal you by prayer, how do you know if it's his will to heal you by medicine? If it's God's will to heal you by medicine, then it's God's will to heal you by prayer.*

If you are not where you can stay away from the doctor,

I'm not against that. I'm just trying to teach you and help you get out of it. If you are going to a doctor for the doctor to help you, don't be saying God put that thing on you. If He did, you better leave it there. Because God said everything that He made was good.

God's not going to make you sick, and then heal you. If He did that, He'd be fighting Himself all the time.

Now let's look at God's work scripturally. Let's forget about what you think about it. Let's forget about what your church has told you. Let's forget about what mama and papa have told you. Let's forget about what the world has told you, because we're Christians. Let's see what our Father says. Because it doesn't make any difference what we think, if it doesn't line up with God's Word then we are wrong. God has never been wrong. God is perfect pure truth.

I JOHN 3:8 says, "FOR THIS PURPOSE THE SON OF GOD WAS MANIFESTED, THAT HE MIGHT DESTROY THE WORKS OF THE DEVIL."

In EXODUS 15:26 He says, "I WILL TAKE SICKNESS AWAY FROM THE MIDST OF THEE." Not give it to you. He says I'll take it away. You may say, "Brother Willis, this is the Old Testament." But if you'll read Hebrews, it says that the Old Testament is a shadow of the New Testament. He's promised to do all that in the Old Testament, but today we can walk in divine health. Most people have a religious computer with about 10 watts in it and we shoot about 20 watts of juice to it and it blows. They just can't take it. But, this is what the Bible says. So, it doesn't make any difference what you think about it; this is the truth.

PSALMS 103:3 says, "HE HEALED ALL OPPRESSED OF THE DEVIL."

I PETER 2:24 says, "BY WHOSE STRIPES YOU WERE HEALED."

"But Brother Willis, why isn't it happening?" Because we've stopped believing. I want to tell you what's happened. The devil's infiltrated and weakened down our churches and the churches have watered the Bible down and are sending people to the doctor. If you don't believe it, get me an invitation to come and preach divine healing in one of your churches and see what happens. If you announce that I'm going to be there, there probably won't be anybody there but me. They'll all have colic that day or something and have to stay home.

Dear Christian friend, God is moving today and is bringing up men and women that will believe the Bible just like He wrote it, and that He'll do just what it says.

I have given you eight scriptures. I can give you plenty more. But the Bible says it will be confirmed in the mouth of two or three witnesses and there are eight. Now you may be standing against this, but you are not standing on the Word against it. You are standing on your old stubborn, bull-headed, hard-headedness.

Jesus wants you to learn how to get your healing from Him. If you believe Jesus heals you can be anywhere in the world and get your healing. Because Jesus is everywhere. But, if you depend upon man the only place you can get your healing is in the doctor's office, or the hospital. But, if you are depending upon Jesus for your healing, you can be in the middle of the desert and get your healing. You can be in the jungles of South America and get your healing. But if you are believing in the doctor and you are out in the middle of the desert, you are up a creek without a paddle. You're going to die.

You know if all the Christians would believe Jesus for their healings, then all the lost people wouldn't have trouble getting a doctor. The doctors would have to pressure off of them. If all the Christians today emptied out of the hospitals and said, "God, I'm going to take you as my healer," they could really start helping the lost people. They'd have time to really do some research work.

Let's look at what Satan's work is. JOB 2:7 says, "SATAN SMOTE JOB WITH BOILS." It's amazing how people say God did that. I know, because I used to teach it that way. The devil just blinds your eyes. The Bible plainly says that Satan smote Job with the boils.

LUKE 13:16 says, "SATAN HATH BOUND, LO THESE EIGHTEEN YEARS." That was the crippled woman. Who bound her? Who put the boils on Job? Satan.

JOHN 8:44 says, "HE WAS A MURDERER FROM THE BEGINNING...HE IS A LIAR, AND THE FATHER OF IT." What does disease do? Who is the murderer? How does he murder? With disease and sickness. It does not say God is a murderer from the beginning. It says Satan is a liar and he is the father of it.

IV. OLD TESTAMENT HEALING (II KINGS 5:1-14)

(1). THE MAN. Verse 1 says he was a captain, he was a great man and he was honorable. It doesn't make any difference who you are, what you are, or your position. The devil has hated you ever since God made you. He's hated man ever since he was made. So, you must realize it doesn't make any difference what your position is. This man was the captain of a great host. He was a great man, successful, well known, and honorable.

(2). THE NEED. He was a leper. It doesn't make any difference how good you are, the devil will load you up with disease. It doesn't make any difference how bad you are, he'll load you up with disease. A lot of us know a lot of good people that are bad off. And we know a lot of wicked people that are bad off. So, it doesn't make any difference. Goodness, morality doesn't keep the devil from saddling people up. If being good and serving God in itself would do it, then a lot of good people wouldn't be sick. I know some good people that the devil has killed.

I want to tell you God doesn't put a heart attack upon a thirty-year-old man and leave a wife with five little kids behind. God is a God of love. That reminds me of a brother that comes to the Center real often. About two years ago he came walking up here and he was a little over 30 years of age with eight children and a bad heart. He was scared he was going to die. They told him he wasn't going to make it and he believed them. I laid my hands on him and said, "Brother, the devil is a stinking liar. God loves you. God will not leave these eight kids to make it the best way they can." Jesus healed that man.

You see a little baby all mangled or crippled and you just can't make me believe that my God, a God of love, did that.

So, it doesn't make any difference who you are, the devil will slap it on you. Ninety-nine per cent of people die of diseases and sickness and every imaginable kind. Most people are brain-washed from the start. They say you get about 40 years of age and start slowing up. They tell you that you get around 50 and start having arthritis. And what's happened to most people? They start having arthritis. They start telling you when you start getting up in years that you get to where you can't sleep very well, and what happens to most people? They get to where they don't sleep.

I want to tell you the devil has trained the world today. But, glory hallelujah, Jesus is in the retraining business.

(3). THE WITNESS. Verse 2 says, "OUT OF THE LAND OF ISRAEL A LITTLE MAID." She was a little maid out of the land of Israel, but she knew that God healed. Won't you go out from this land of Israel and tell people that Jesus heals? Verse 3 says, "SHE SAID UNTO HER MISTRESS." She was bold enough to speak to her mistress. I want to encourage you to be a witness. There are not very many people that know God heals. And most of you are not bold enough to tell them. God wants to raise you up so you'll begin to tell people that Jesus heals. As you begin to tell them, then Jesus will start healing some of them. It doesn't make any difference who you are, tell people that Jesus saves and heals.

We have a sister that's 73 years old and that young lady has brought in about 20 or 30 people that have gotten saved. You know the world says when you get 70 you can't do much any more. She didn't start coming to the Center until after she was 70 herself. We have a lot of brothers and sister 65 or 70 years old and if you'll learn this healing message you'll be around for a long time. But, if you listen to the world your days are short. The Bible says in Psalms, He promises you three score and ten. That's 70. He says in I Corinthians all the promises of God are yea and amen. "But, Brother Willis, a lot of people are going out before they are 70. Why?" They don't believe in it, and you can't get anything from God that you don't believe. If He's promised heaven and that's real, then three score and ten is real also. He says everything above that's grace. I believe in grace.

(4). THE PROBLEM. The little maid told Naaman and do you know what he did? He went to the King. That would be just like some of you going to your church here and saying, "Would you anoint me with oil to be healed?" They'd say, "That's what God put doctors here for."

He went to this king and the king said, "Who do you think I am?" He said, "You're seeking to have a quarrel with me." You go ask your preacher to anoint you with oil and pray for you to be healed and cast devils out of you and he'll say, "What are you trying to do? Get me run off? You know that we Methodists don't teach that. We Baptists don't believe in that. We Catholics don't believe in that." I agree with you. The Methodists don't. The Baptists don't. The Catholics don't. The Presbyterians don't. But, the Bible does. The Bible says it.

Many of God's people don't know what to do. They go to man. The first time I heard Norvel Hayes about four years ago up in Jackson, Mississippi, he said if you are sick and your church doesn't believe in healing, go where they do believe. If you need deliverance, and your church doesn't believe in casting out devils, go where they do believe. He said, "People come up to me and say, "My church doesn't believe in divine healing" and I say, "Stay there and die. Or go where they do believe in it."

If somebody would tell you right now that there was a doctor in China that could heal your disease, you'd sell your house, you'd do everything to get over there. And Jesus says He'll heal you anywhere. "But I don't believe that." But, you'd go to China to see a man.

When we were young we heard about doctors all over the country that could do something for our son, Lynn. We went everywhere. Anytime they'd tell us about some doctor that maybe could do something that would help our son, we took off. Lynn had been in school since he was three years of age, and he's 23 now. About three years ago I was sitting in the barber chair in Jeanerette, Louisiana, and Lynn was home for a few days from Pinecrest, and he had just got through getting his hair cut. The Holy Ghost spoke to me and said "If you'll bring him home, I'll heal him." And, of course, the devil said, "You're stupid."

You know I went up there to Pinecrest to get him out and the people didn't want to let him out. They said, "Well, we've had other people get excited about these things you know, and take their children out and later be sorry for it."

And, I said, "I want to bring him out." So, they put him out on a furlough. I couldn't get them to drop him right then. So, finally, just to keep from debating with them, I let them put him on a year's furlough. A year later I got a letter saying if I didn't bring him back in 30 days, I would not be able to bring him back. And I just threw it away. I want to tell you that young man has been a light in our home. And, by faith, he's healed from the top of his head to the bottom of his feet. I'm speaking that in faith, and God's going to make it a fact.

Naaman went to the wrong place. Do you want to know why a lot of people are dying today? They are going to man and not to God. There are a lot of Bible examples about this. He took ten talents of silver, six thousand pieces of gold, and ten changes of raiment. People think their money can get it for them. Faith in Jesus Christ is worth more than money when you're sick.

(5). THE INSTRUCTIONS. He went to the King of Israel and the King couldn't do him any good. But, they got the word to him about the prophet Elisha. Finally, he went down to the prophet and knocked on the door and being a great man, expected Elisha to come out to him. Elisha just sent his servant out there and said, "Tell him to go wash in the Jordan seven times and he shall be clean."

(6). THE RESPONSE. The scriptures say he was wroth, he was angry. He thought surely he ought to do more than that. Now, it's ridiculous to the natural mind to say go wash in the river Jordan seven times. Naaman believed it. Oh he got angry. But, he believed.

(7). THE OBEDIENCE & REWARD. Naaman was obedient. In verse 14 it says he went; he dipped seven times in the Jordan, according to the saying of the man of God. "And he was clean."

What I'm simply saying to you is this, man went and obeyed God's man. I just want you to obey God's Word.

MARK 16:16 says "HE THAT BELIEVETH AND IS BAPTIZED SHALL BE SAVED; BUT HE THAT BELIEVETH NOT SHALL BE DAMNED. AND THESE SIGNS SHALL FOLLOW THEM THAT BELIEVE, IN MY NAME SHALL THEY CAST OUT DEVILS; THEY SHALL SPEAK IN TONGUES; THEY SHALL TAKE UP SERPENTS; AND IF THEY DRINK ANY DEADLY THING, IT SHALL NOT HURT THEM; THEY SHALL LAY THEIR HANDS ON THE SICK, AND THEY SHALL RECOVER."

I believe the Word of God, don't you? It says we'll lay our hands on the sick and they shall recover.